ACKNOWLEDGMENTS

The Rules Commission and USA Volleyball would like to express their appreciation to the many individuals and organizations for their assistance in the editing of and providing information for this publication.

Special thanks go to Brian Hemelgarn, Stephen Shepherd, Julie Voeck, Rachael Stringer, and Cindy Compoc for their support and knowledge in the development of this publication.

FIVB™

Rules of the Game as authorized by the International Volleyball Federation (FIVB) at the 35th FIVB Congress, Buenos Aires, Argentina, 2016 and amended.

Published by USA Volleyball.

USAVolleyball

USA Volleyball has officially approved the modifications presented in this document in order to promote the sport and encourage continuity of play at the various organizational, local and recreational levels across the country.

This abridged version of the USA Volleyball 2019-2021 Indoor Rules Book emphasizes these modifications and does not include FIVB rules that are not in effect for USAV competition. Rules changes that have been approved for the 2019-2021 seaons are highlighted in gray.

For the official international rules of the game, which are used worldwide and developed and approved by the FIVB, please visit www.fivb.org or our web site at www.usavolleyball.org.

USA Volleyball embraces this view, joining with all of its global partners to enable pleasurable participation from the broadest base of recreational play, to the highest levels of international competition.

Volleyball can enrich the lives of all who play and watch it. It should be fun.

WE COMMIT THE RULES TO THIS END.

This publication is available on the USA Volleyball website.

4065 Sinton Rd, Suite 200 Colorado Springs, Colorado 80907
Phone: (719) 228-6800
Fax: (719) 228-6899
postmaster@usav.org

ISBN: 978-1-7332851-2-4

TABLE OF CONTENTS

SECTION I

ORDER OF THE RULES
THE GAME

CHAPTER 1
FACILITIES AND EQUIPMENT

CHAPTER 2
PARTICIPANTS

CHAPTER 3
PLAYING FORMAT

CHAPTER 4
PLAYING ACTIONS

CHAPTER 5
INTERRUPTIONS, DELAYS AND INTERVALS

TABLE OF CONTENTS

SECTION I

ORDER OF THE RULES

THE GAME

USAVolleyball

CHAPTER 1
FACILITIES AND EQUIPMENT

RULE 1. PLAYING AREA

The playing area includes the playing court and the free zone. It shall be rectangular and symmetrical.

1.1 DIMENSIONS

The playing court is a rectangle measuring 18 x 9 m (59' x 29'6") surrounded by a free zone which is a minimum of 3 m (9'10") wide on all sides.

The free playing space is the space above the playing area which is free from any obstructions. The free playing space shall measure a minimum of 7 m (23') in height from the playing surface.

a. The playing court is a rectangle measuring 18 x 9 m (59' x 29'6") surrounded by a free zone, which may be a minimum of 2 m (6'6 3/4"). It is not required that the free zone be symmetrical.

b. The free playing space is the space above the playing area which is free from any obstructions. For nationally sanctioned competition and recommended for all other competitions, 7 m (23') is the minimum free playing space (ceiling height).

1.2 PLAYING SURFACE

1.2.1 The surface must be flat, horizontal and uniform. It must not present any danger of injury to the players. It is forbidden to play on rough or slippery surfaces.

a. Players may mop the floor provided the 1st referee does not judge the action to be a delay.

b. For nationally sanctioned competition, USA Volleyball must approve the surface.

1.2.2 On indoor courts the surface of the playing court must be of a light color.

It is recommended when using a portable playing surface that the color of the playing court be contrasting to that of the free zone.

1.2.3 On outdoor courts a slope of 5 mm per meter is allowed for drainage. Court lines made of solid materials are forbidden.

1.3 LINES ON THE COURT

1.3.1 All lines are 5 cm (2") wide. They must be of a light color which is different from the color of the floor and from any other lines.

Lines are not required to be of a light color as long as they contrast with the color of the floor.

1.3.2 Boundary lines

Two sidelines and two end lines mark the playing court. Both sidelines and end lines are drawn inside the dimensions of the playing court.

1.3.3 Center line

The axis of the center line divides the playing court into two equal courts measuring 9 x 9 m (29'6" x 29'6") each; however, the entire width of the line is considered to belong to both courts equally. This line extends beneath the net from sideline to sideline.

1.3.4 Attack line

On each court, an attack line, whose rear edge is drawn 3 m (9'10") back from the axis of the center line, marks the front zone.

For nationally sanctioned competitions, the extensions of the attack lines outside the court are required as described above. These extensions are optional for all other events. The coach's restriction line is optional for all events.

1.4 ZONES AND AREAS

1.4.1 Front zone

On each court the front zone is limited by the axis of the center line and the rear edge of the attack line.

The front zone is considered to extend beyond the sidelines to the end of the free zone.

1.4.2 Service zone

The service zone is a 9 m (29'6") wide area behind each end line.

It is laterally limited by two short lines, each 15 cm (6") long, drawn 20 cm (8") behind the end line as an extension of the sidelines. Both short lines are included in the width of the service zone.

In depth, the service zone shall have a minimum depth of 2 m (6'6 3/4"). If this zone is less than 2 m (6'6 3/4"), a line shall be marked on the court to provide the minimum depth. After the service, the line is ignored and becomes part of the court.

1.4.3 Substitution zone

The substitution zone is limited by the extension of both attack lines up to the scorer's table.

1.4.4 Libero Replacement Zone

The Libero Replacement Zone is part of the free zone on the side of the team benches, limited by the extension of the attack line up to the end line.

1.4.5 Warm-up area

The warm-up area is at the end of the bench or bench area, and no nearer to the court than the front of the team bench. Substitutes must not interfere with play or the officials' duties.

1.4.6 Penalty Area

A penalty area, sized approximately 1 x 1 m (39" x 39") and equipped with two chairs, is located in the control area, outside the prolongation of each end line. They may be limited by a 5 cm (2") wide red line.

Inclusion of a penalty area as described above is recommended.

1.5 TEMPERATURE

The minimum temperature shall not be below 10° C (50° F).

1.6 LIGHTING

For nationally sanctioned USA Volleyball competition, the lighting on the playing area should be 300 lux (27.9 foot candles) measured at 1 m (39") above the playing surface.

RULE 2. NET AND POSTS

2.1 HEIGHT OF THE NET

2.1.1 Placed vertically over the center line there is a net. The height of the net may vary for specific age groups as follows:

Age Groups	Female/Reverse Co-Ed	Male/Co-Ed
70 years and above	2.19 m (7'2 1/8")	2.29 m (7'6")
55 years and above	2.19 m (7'2 1/8")	2.38 m (7'9 5/8")
45 years and above	2.19 m (7'2 1/8")	2.43 m (7'11 5/8")
15/18 years and under	2.24 m (7'4 1/8")	2.43 m (7'11 5/8")
13/14 years and under	2.24 m (7'4 1/8")	2.24 m (7'4 1/8")
11/12 years and under	2.13 m (7'0")	2.13 m (7'0")
10 years and under	1.98 m (6'6")	2.13 m (7'0")

2.1.2 Its height is measured from the center of the playing court. The net height (over the two sidelines) must be exactly the same and must not exceed the official height bymore than 2 cm (3/4").

2.2 STRUCTURE

The net is 39" (1 m) wide and 31'6"-33' (9.50 to 10 m) long (with 10"-19 1/2" [25 to 50 cm] on each side of the side bands), made of 4" (10 cm) square black mesh.

At its top a horizontal band 2" to 2 3/4" (5 to 7 cm) wide, made of two-fold white canvas, is sewn along its full length.

Within the band, a flexible cable fastens the net to the posts and keeps its top taut. At the bottom of the net there is another horizontal band, 2" (5 cm) wide, similar to the top band, through which is threaded a rope. This rope fastens the net to the posts and keeps its lower part taut.

2.3 SIDE BANDS

Two white bands are fastened vertically to the net and placed directly above each sideline.

They are 5 cm (2") wide and 1 m (39") long and are considered as part of the net.

The side bands as described above are optional.

2.4 ANTENNAE

An antenna is a flexible rod, 5’11” (1.80 m) long and 3/8” (10 mm) in diameter, made of fiberglass or similar material. An antenna is fastened at the outer edge of each side band. The antennae are placed on opposite sides of the net. The top 32” (80 cm) of each antenna extends above the net and is marked with 4” (10 cm) stripes of contrasting color, preferably red and white. The antennae are considered as part of the net and laterally delimit the crossing space.

2.5 POSTS

2.5.1 The posts supporting the net are placed at a distance of 0.50-1.00 m (20”-39”) outside the sidelines. They are 2.55 m (8’4”) high and preferably adjustable.

2.5.2 The posts are rounded and smooth, fixed to the ground without wires. There shall be no dangerous or obstructing devices.

Ceiling mounted net systems are allowed.

2.6 ADDITIONAL EQUIPMENT

a. If the posts are secured by barrels or other supporting apparatus, there must be some means of clearly identifying the barrels or supporting apparatus. All other dangerous or obstructing devices must be eliminated. Metal cables, tensioning devices and other exposed wires may need to be covered if the referees determine these items may cause injury to players.

b. All wires that support posts from the floor will be eliminated, or if that is not possible, then all exposed wires must be padded with at least 1.25 cm (1/2”) thick, resilient, shock-absorbing material throughout the entire length. The padding must be clearly recognizable.

c. Posts shall be padded to a minimum height of 1.7 m (5’6”) with at least 1.25 cm (1/2”) thick, resilient, shock-absorbing material throughout the entire length. The padding must be clearly recognizable.

d. Basic equipment includes a referee stand, which should be adjustable to allow the referee’s eye position to be approximately 50 cm (19”) above the top of the net. It should be constructed so that it presents the least potential hazard for participants. Step ladders, jump boxes and other devices not specifically designed as referee stands shall not be used. If an appropriate referee stand cannot be provided, the 1st referee performs his/her functions from the floor.

e. The front and sides of the referee’s stand must be padded in the same manner as the posts to a height of 1.7 m (5’6”).

f. The scoreboard must be divided into two separate parts with numbers that provide the score for each team. The score displayed on the scoreboard is not official and may not be used as a basis for protest.

RULE 3. BALLS

3.1 STANDARDS

The ball shall be spherical, made of a flexible leather or synthetic leather case with a bladder inside, made of rubber or a similar material.

Its color may be a uniform light color or a combination of colors.

Its circumference is 65-67 cm (25.6” to 26.4”) and its weight is 260-280 g (9 to 10 oz).

Its inside pressure shall be 0.30 to 0.325 kg/cm2 (4.26 to 4.61 psi) (294.3 to 318.82 mbar or hPa).

Twelve-and-under competition at the USAV Junior National Championships will be conducted using a ball with the same circumference and inside pressure as listed in Rule 3.1, but with a weight of 198 to 227 g (7 to 8 oz).

3.2 UNIFORMITY OF BALLS

All balls used in a match must have the same standards regarding circumference, weight, pressure, type, color, etc.

CHAPTER 2
PARTICIPANTS

RULE 4. TEAMS

4.1 TEAM COMPOSITION

4.1.1

a. Players are the team members on the court. Substitutes are team members in uniform who are not in the starting line-up of a set.

b. A team may consist of a maximum of 15 players and five coaches/team personnel (unless modified by the Specific Competition Regulations). An American Sign Language (ASL) interpreter may be included among the coaching staff or team personnel; see ASL Interpreter Guidelines.

c. A complete junior team consists of a minimum of six players and a USAV certified juniors' coach.

4.1.2 One of the players is the team captain, who shall be indicated on the score sheet.

The Libero may be team or game captain.

4.1.3 Only the players recorded on the tournament entry form/roster may enter the court and play in the match.

When rosters are utilized, each team shall submit a roster listing the names and uniform numbers of players eligible to participate in the match at least 10 minutes before the start of each match, including tournament play. The coach or team captain must sign the roster. A roster may be changed at any time during the match, but only to correct a uniform number. However, if the coach or game captain requests such a number change, that team will be charged with a penalty point. A roster may not be changed to add a player at any time after having been signed by the coach or team captain.

4.2 LOCATION OF THE TEAM

4.2.1 The players not in play should either sit on their team bench or be in their warm-up area. The location of the coach and one assistant coach is defined in Rules 5.2 and 5.3 below; all other team members sit on the bench but may temporarily leave it. The benches for the teams are located beside the scorer's table, outside the free zone.

In conjunction with rule 4.2.1 above, any team member may occupy any available seat on their team's bench, including the first chair reserved for the coach.

4.2.2 Only the team composition members are permitted to sit on the bench during the match and to participate in the official warm-up session.

4.2.3 Players not in play may warm up without balls as follows:

4.2.3.1 during play: in the warm-up areas;

4.2.3.2 during time-outs and technical time-outs: in the free zone behind their court.

4.2.4 During set intervals, players may warm up using balls on their court or in their free zone.

4.3 EQUIPMENT

A player's uniform consists of a jersey and shorts or athletic pants/sports pants. If undergarments, including but not limited to T-shirts, boxer shorts, tights, leotards, body suits, bicycle shorts, sports bras, etc., are worn in such a manner that they are exposed, they will be considered a part of the uniform. In that case, they must be similar and the same color for any team members (except the Libero) who wear such a uniform. Socks and sport shoes are not part of the uniform.

The legality of a team's uniform(s) is not grounds for a protest by their opponent. The determination of a team's uniform legality is the responsibility of the match referee(s), head referee(s), and/or tournament staff.

4.3.1 The uniforms must be clean.

The color and design for the jerseys and shorts or athletic pants/sports pants must be uniform for the team (except for the Libero).

4.3.2 The shoes must be light and pliable with rubber or composite soles without heels.

4.3.3 The players' jerseys must be numbered in a permanent manner from 1 to 99 using Arabic numerals.

Duplicate numbers and leading zeroes (i.e., 01, 02, etc.) are not allowed.

4.3.3.1 The color and brightness of the numbers must contrast with the color and brightness of the jerseys.

a. Uniform numbers must be clearly visible and centered (both horizontally and vertically) on the player's chest and upper back.
b. Each jersey must use the same color and number height for all players, except the Libero's jersey, which may have different color and size numbers, provided it still meets the minimum criteria stated in USAV 4.3.3.2.
c. Color combinations such as purple/black, dark green/black, navy/black, white/light yellow or navy/maroon are not distinctive enough to comply with the rules.
d. The color of the number must clearly contrast with the color of the jersey irrespective of any border around the number.

4.3.3.2 The stripe forming the numbers shall be a minimum of 3/4" (2 cm) in width.

The numbers must be a minimum of 4" (10 cm) in height on the chest and a minimum of 6" (15 cm) in height on the back. It is recommended that the numbers be a minimum of 6" (15 cm) in height on the chest and a minimum of 8" (20 cm) on the back.

4.3.5 Uniforms must be identical with the exception of sleeve length and the Libero players. An exception will also be made for a single manufacturer's logo or trademark on the outside of the jerseys or shorts, provided that the logo or trademark does not exceed 2 1/4 square inches (14.6 square cm). Sponsor logos are permitted provided they are identical on each uniform and do not obstruct the view of the uniform number.

4.4 CHANGE OF EQUIPMENT

The 1st referee may authorize one or more players:

4.4.1 to play barefoot;

4.4.2 to change wet or damaged uniforms between sets or after substitution, provided that the color, design and number of the new uniform(s) are the same,

4.4.3 to play in training suits in cold weather, provided that they are of the same color and design for the whole team (except for the Liberos) and numbered according to Rule 4.3.3.

4.5 FORBIDDEN OBJECTS

4.5.1 It is forbidden to wear objects which may cause injury or give an artificial advantage to the player.

It is forbidden to wear hats or casts (even if padded). Braces, prosthetic limbs or other headgear that may cause an injury or give an artificial advantage to the player must not be worn. If a brace, prosthetic limb or headgear is used, padding or covering may be necessary. Jewelry may be worn provided its nature does not present a concern for safety, such as extremely long necklaces and/ or necklaces with large medallions, or large hoop earrings.

4.5.2 Players may wear glasses or lenses at their own risk.

If a player's equipment falls to the floor and creates a safety hazard, play is stopped, and a delay sanction may be assessed.

4.5.3 Compression pads (padded injury protection devices) may be worn for protection or support.

RULE 5. TEAM LEADERS

Both the team captain and the coach are responsible for the conduct and discipline of their team members.

The Libero may be team or game captain.

5.1 CAPTAIN

5.1.1 The captain does not sign the score sheet before the match.

5.1.2 DURING THE MATCH and while on the court, the team captain is the game captain. When the team captain is not on the court, the coach or the team captain must assign another player on the court to assume the role of game captain. This game captain maintains his/ her responsibilities until he/she is substituted or replaced, or the team captain returns to play, or the set ends.

When the ball is out of play, only the game captain is authorized to speak to the referees:

5.1.2.1 to ask for an explanation on the application or interpretation of the Rules, and also to submit the requests or questions of his/her teammates.

If an explanation of an application or interpretation of a rule is not satisfactory to the game captain, he/she must immediately indicate his/her disagreement and file an official protest prior to the authorization of the next service. If the disagreement with the referees' explanation involves the last point of the set, the official protest must be recorded within the first 60 seconds of the timed interval between sets. If the final point of the match is disputed, the protest must be recorded within the first 60 seconds after the final point of the match is scored. (Protest is ruled upon by the Championship Committee either immediately or prior to the start of the next set.) It is advisable to have an assigned Protest Committee available to rule upon a protest as soon as possible prior to the first service following the protest. Such action should preclude playing the match over from the point of protest if the protest is upheld. Protests considered by the 1st referee (Protest or Tournament Committee) include a: 1) misinterpretation of a playing rule, 2) failure of the 1st referee to apply the correct rule to a given situation, 3) failure to charge the correct penalty-sanction for a given fault, or 4) a scoring discrepancy. Protest facts recorded on the score sheet include the: 1) score of the set at the time of the protest, 2) players and positions at the time of the protest, 3) player substitutions and team substitutions made up to the protest, 4) team time-outs taken up to the protest, 5) situation that caused the protest, and 6) signatures of the scorer, captains and 1st referee, indicating the facts are correct.

5.1.2.2 to ask authorization:

a. to change all or part of the equipment;
b. to verify the positions of the teams;
c. to check the floor, the net, the ball, etc.;

For nationally sanctioned competition, the coach may act in place of the game captain to perform the functions stated in 5.1.2.1 and 5.1.2.2. The coach is not permitted to cross the court to speak with the 1st referee. The 1st referee may leave the stand to address a coach near the team bench, if necessary, when a certified professional 2nd referee is not assigned to the match.

5.1.3 AT THE END OF THE MATCH, the team captain thanks the referees but does not sign the score sheet.

5.2 COACH

5.2.1 Throughout the match, the coach conducts the play of his/her team from outside the playing court. He/she selects the starting line-ups, the substitutes, and takes time-outs. In these functions his/her contacting official is the 2nd referee.

5.2.3 DURING THE MATCH, the coach:

5.2.3.1 prior to each set, gives the 2nd referee or the scorer the line-up sheet(s) duly filled in and signed;

5.2.3.2 may sit anywhere on the team bench and may also stand or walk in the team bench area as described in USAV 5.2.3.4 below;

5.2.3.3 requests time-outs and substitutions;

is also authorized to speak to the referees to verify the positions of the teams;

5.2.3.4 may, as well as other team members, give instructions to the players on the court. The coach may give these instructions while standing or walking within the free zone in front of his/her team's bench from the extension of the attack line up to the warm-up area, without disturbing or delaying the match.

During play, the coach may give these instructions while standing or walking within the free zone in front of his/her team's bench from the extension of the attack line up to and including the warm-up area, no closer to the court than 1.75 m (5'10") from the sideline and its extension without disturbing or delaying the match. The extension of the attack line is drawn to a distance of 1.75 m (5'10") from the sideline.

5.3 ASSISTANT COACH

5.3.1 One assistant coach at a time may stand to give instructions to the players on the court but has no right to intervene in the match. During play, the assistant coach may give these instructions while standing or walking within the free zone in front of his/her team's bench from the extension of the attack line up to and including the warm-up area, and no closer to the court than 1.75 m (5'10") from the sideline and its extension, without disturbing or delaying the match. The extension of the attack line is drawn to a distance of 1.75 m (5'10") from the sideline.

5.3.2 Should the coach have to leave his/her team for any reason including sanction, but excluding entering the court as a player, an assistant coach may assume the coach's functions for the duration of the absence, once confirmed to the referee by the game captain.

CHAPTER 3
PLAYING FORMAT

RULE 6. TO SCORE A POINT, TO WIN A SET AND THE MATCH

6.1 TO SCORE A POINT

6.1.1 Point

A team scores a point:

6.1.1.1 by successfully landing the ball on the opponent's court;

6.1.1.2 when the opponent team commits a fault;

6.1.1.3 when the opponent team receives a penalty.

6.1.2 Fault

A team commits a fault by making a playing action contrary to the rules (or by violating them in some other way). The referees judge the faults and determine the consequences according to the Rules:

6.1.2.1 If two or more faults are committed successively, only the first one is counted.

6.1.2.2 If two or more faults are committed by opponents simultaneously, a DOUBLE FAULT is called and the rally is replayed.

6.1.3 Rally and completed rally

A rally is the sequence of playing actions from the moment of the service hit by the server until the ball is out of play. A completed rally is the sequence of playing actions which results in the award of a point.

This includes:

- the award of a penalty
- loss of service for service hit made after the time limit.

6.1.3.1 If the serving team wins a rally, it scores a point and continues to serve.

6.1.3.2 If the receiving team wins a rally, it scores a point and it must serve next.

6.2 TO WIN A SET

A set (except the deciding 5th set) is won by the team which first scores 25 points with a minimum lead of two points. In the case of a 24-24 tie, play is continued until a two-point lead is achieved (26-24; 27-25; etc.).

6.3 TO WIN THE MATCH

6.3.1 For tournament play, the match is won by the team that wins two sets out of three. A set (except the deciding 3rd set) is won by the first team to score 25 points with a minimum lead of two points.

6.3.2 In the case of a 1- tie, the deciding 3rd set is played to 15 points with a minimum lead of 2 points.

6.3.3 A playoff set is considered a match and only one set will be played. The match is won by the team that scores either 15 or 25 (as specified in the tournament guidelines) with a two-point advantage. Teams change courts when one team has scored 8 or 13 points, respectively.

6.4 DEFAULT AND INCOMPLETE TEAM

6.4.1 If a team refuses to play after being summoned to do so, it is declared in default and forfeits the match with the result 0-2 for the match and 0-25 for each set.

6.4.2 A team that, without justifiable reason, does not appear on the playing court on time is declared in default with the same result as in Rule 6.4.1.

If failure to adhere to Rule 6.4.2 is due to insufficient players on a team to begin a match, the team forfeits the first set at match time. After a team forfeits the first set of a match, an interval of up to 10 minutes shall be allowed for the team to produce sufficient players to play the next set. If the team is complete (per USAV 4.1.1c) prior to the expiration of this interval, the late team will be permitted use of the full court for a four-minute warm-up before play begins. If, after the 10-minute interval the team is not complete, the second set shall be declared a forfeit. If the match consists of the best three out of five sets, an additional 10-minute interval shall be allowed before the match is declared a forfeit.

6.4.3 A team that is declared INCOMPLETE for the set or for the match, loses the set or the match. The opponent team is given the points, or the points and the sets, needed to win the set or the match. The incomplete team keeps its points and sets.

Matches that are two sets out of three will have a match result of 0-2 or 1-2 depending when the default occurs.

RULE 7. STRUCTURE OF PLAY

7.1 THE TOSS

Before the match, the 1st referee carries out a toss to decide upon the first service and the sides of the court in the first set. If a deciding set is to be played, a new toss will be carried out.

7.1.1 The toss is taken in the presence of the two team captains. Multiple team representatives may attend the captains' meeting with the team captain. The 1st referee will confirm which player will represent the team for the toss.

7.1.2 The winner of the toss chooses: EITHER

7.1.2.1 the right to serve or to receive the service,

OR

7.1.2.2 the side of the court.

The loser takes the remaining choice.

7.2 OFFICIAL WARM-UP SESSION

7.2.1 Unless modified, the teams are entitled to a 10-minute official warm-up period consisting of two minutes of shared court, followed by two 4-minute periods of exclusive use.

7.2.2

a. For consecutive warm-up periods, the team with first service has the court first.

b. For junior competition, when one team has exclusive use of the court, the other team must either be at its team bench or out of the playing area. Warming up with balls at the team bench or in the spectator walkways is not permitted, even if other aspects of the warm-up period are modified. Retrieving balls for the opponents during their warm-up period is allowed.

7.3 TEAM STARTING LINE-UP

7.3.1 There must always be six players per team in play. The team's starting line-up indicates the rotational order of the players on the court. This order must be maintained throughout the set.

7.3.2 At least two minutes before the end of the timed warm-up period and 30 seconds prior to the expiration of the interval between sets, a coach or game captain submits the team's starting line-up on a signed line-up sheet to the 2nd referee or scorer.

7.3.3 The players who are not in the starting line-up of a set are the substitutes for that set (except the Liberos).

7.3.4 Once a line-up has been submitted, no changes may be made without a regular substitution. However, if a team submits a line-up sheet that lists a player's number as both a Libero and as a starting player, the coach or captain shall immediately decide whether that player will be a Libero or a starting player. If the duplicate number will be a Libero, the coach must correct the line-up but only in the starting position where the Libero's number was recorded. If the duplicate number will be the starting player, another player may immediately be designated as Libero. The team will not be charged a substitution.

7.3.5 Discrepancies between players' position on court and on the line-up sheet are dealt with as follows:

7.3.5.1 When such a discrepancy is discovered before the start of the set, players' positions must be rectified according to those on the line-up sheet––there will be no sanction;

7.3.5.2 when, before the start of the set, any player on court is found not to be registered on the line-up sheet of that set, this player must be changed to conform to the line-up sheet–– there will be no sanction;

7.3.5.3 however, if the coach wishes to keep such non-recorded player(s) on the court, he/she has to request regular substitution(s), by use of the corresponding hand signal, which will then be recorded on the score sheet. If a discrepancy between players' positions and the line-up sheet is discovered later, the team at fault must revert to the correct positions. The opponent's points remain valid and in addition they receive a point and the next service.

If the positional fault is discovered before the opponent serves, all points scored subsequent to the fault must be cancelled. In addition, all time-outs taken by the team not a fault, as well as substitutions and team sanctions charged to either team subsequent to the commission of the positional fault, must be cancelled. Individual misconduct sanctions assessed to either team, and time-outs taken by the team at fault, are not cancelled. If the points scored while the player was out of position cannot be determined or the opponents have served, a loss of rally is the only penalty. The opponents retain any points scored.

7.3.5.4 Where a player is found to be on court but he/she is not registered on the team roster, the opponent's points remain valid, and in addition they gain a point and service. The team at fault will lose all points and/or sets (0:25, if necessary) gained from the moment the non-registered player entered the court, and will have to submit a revised line-up sheet and send a new registered player into the court, in the position of the non-registered player.

7.4 POSITIONS

At the moment the ball is hit by the server, each team must be positioned within its own court in the rotational order (except the server).

7.4.1 The positions of the players are numbered as follows:

7.4.1.1 The three players along the net are front-row players and occupy positions 4 (front-left), 3 (front-center) and 2 (front-right);

7.4.1.2 The other three are back-row players occupying positions 5 (back-left), 6 (back-center) and 1 (back-right).

7.4.2 Relative positions between players:

7.4.2.1 Each back-row player must be positioned further back from the center line than the corresponding front-row player;

7.4.2.2 The front-row players and the back-row players, respectively, must be positioned laterally in the order indicated in Rule 7.4.1.

7.4.3 The positions of players are determined and controlled according to the positions of their feet contacting the ground as follows:

7.4.3.1 each front-row player must have at least a part of his/her foot closer to the center line than the feet of the corresponding back-row player;

7.4.3.2 each right- (left-) side player must have at least a part of his/ her foot closer to the right (left) sideline than the feet of the center player in that row.

The position of the players is judged according to the position of the foot last in contact with the floor at the time the ball is contacted for service.

7.4.4 After the service hit, the players may move around and occupy any position on their court and the free zone.

7.5 POSITIONAL FAULT

7.5.1 The team commits a positional fault, if any player is not in his/her correct position at the moment the ball is hit by the server. When a player is on court through illegal substitution, and play restarts, this is counted as a positional fault with the consequences of an illegal substitution.

7.5.2 If the server commits a serving fault at the moment of the service hit, the server's fault is counted before a positional fault.

7.5.3 If the service becomes faulty after the service hit, it is the positional fault that will be counted.

7.5.4 A positional fault leads to the following consequences:

7.5.4.1 the team is sanctioned with a point and service to the opponent;

7.5.4.2 players' positions must be rectified.

If the positional fault is discovered before the opponent serves, all points scored subsequent to the fault must be cancelled. In addition, all time-outs taken by the team not at fault, as well as substitutions and team sanctions charged to either team subsequent to the commission of the positional fault, must be cancelled. Individual misconduct sanctions assessed to either team and time-outs taken by the team at fault, are not cancelled. If the points scored while the player was out of position cannot be determined or the opponents have served, then a loss of rally is the only penalty charged. The opponents retain any points scored.

7.6 ROTATION

7.6.1 The rotational order is determined by the team's starting line-up and controlled with the service order and players' positions throughout the set.

7.6.2 When the receiving team has gained the right to serve, its players rotate one position clockwise: the player in position 2 rotates to position 1 to serve, the player in position 1 rotates to position 6, etc.

7.7 ROTATIONAL FAULT

7.7.1 A rotational fault is committed when the SERVICE is not made according to the rotational order or when a Libero serves in a second rotation position in the same set. It leads to the following consequences in order:

7.7.1.1 the scorer stops play by the buzzer; the opponent gains a point and next service. If the rotational fault is determined only after the completion of the rally which started with a rotational fault, only a single point is awarded to the opponent, regardless of the result of the rally played.

7.7.1.2 the rotational order of the faulty team must be rectified;

7.7.2 Additionally, the scorer should determine the exact moment when the fault was committed, and all points scored subsequently by the team at fault must be cancelled. The opponent's points remain valid. If that moment cannot be determined, no point(s) cancellation takes place, and a point and service to the opponent is the only sanction.

If the rotational fault is discovered before the opponents serve, all points scored subsequent to the fault must be cancelled. In addition, all time-outs taken by the team not at fault, as well as substitutions and team sanctions charged to either team subsequent to the commission of the rotational fault, must be cancelled. Individual misconduct sanctions assessed to either team, and time-outs taken by the team at fault, are not cancelled. If the points scored while the player was out of rotation cannot be determined or the opponents have served, then a point and service to the opponents is the only penalty charged. The opponents retain any points scored.

CHAPTER 4
PLAYING ACTIONS

RULE 8. STATES OF PLAY

8.1 BALL IN PLAY

The ball is in play from the moment of the hit of the service authorized by the 1st referee.

8.2 BALL OUT OF PLAY

The ball is out of play at the moment of the fault which is whistled by one of the referees; in the absence of a fault, at the moment of the whistle.

In the case of an inadvertent whistle, the rally is ended. The 1st referee must make a ruling that will not penalize either team.

8.3 BALL "IN"

The ball is "in" if at any moment of its contact with the floor, some part of the ball touches the court, including the boundary lines.

8.4 BALL "OUT"

The ball is "out" when:

8.4.1 all parts of the ball which contact the floor are completely outside the boundary lines;

8.4.2 it touches an object outside the court, the ceiling or a person out of play;

A ball, other than a served ball, shall remain in play if it contacts the ceiling or other overhead objects 4.6 m (15') or more above the playing area.

a. If benches, bleachers, low-hanging baskets or other floor obstructions are less than 2 m (6'6 3/4") from the court and interfere with play of the ball, the ball becomes out of play and a replay may be directed at the 1st referee's discretion.

b. The ball is out of play when:

   i. Rule 10.1.2 is not in effect, and the ball makes contact with the ceiling or obstruction above the opponent's playing area.

   ii. Rule 10.1.2 is in effect, and a ball that cannot be legally retrieved from the opponent's free zone contacts the ceiling or obstruction over the opponent's playing area.

   iii. The ball contacts the ceiling or obstruction above the team's playing area and crosses the plane of the net into the opponent's court.

   iv. The ball contacts the ceiling or any obstruction after the team's third hit.

c. A ball, other than a served ball, is out of play and a replay directed if it contacts overhead object(s) or the supports (e.g., basketball backboard) less than 4.6 m (15') above the playing area and would have remained playable if the object had not been present.

d. A ball is out of play if it contacts the ceiling or overhead objects, regardless of height, over non-playing areas.

e. A ball is out of play and a replay is directed if the ball comes to rest on an overhead object above the team's playing area and is still a playable ball.

f. If an official, media equipment or personnel or spectator interferes with a player's legal attempt to play the ball over the playing area, a replay shall be directed.

8.4.3. it touches the antennae, ropes, posts or the net itself outside the side bands;

8.4.4. it crosses the vertical plane of the net either partially or totally outside the crossing space, except in the case of Rule 10.1.2;

8.4.5. it crosses completely the lower space under the net.

RULE 9. PLAYING THE BALL

Each team must play within its own playing area and space (except Rule 10.1.2). The ball may be retrieved from beyond the free zone when the surface change is 1.25 cm (1/2") or less, the secondary surface is lower than the free zone and the area is free of obstructions. If obstructions or other safety concerns prohibit retrieval from beyond the free zone, the player retrieving a ball over a non-playing area must be in contact with the playing surface when contact with the ball is made.

Non-playing areas are defined as the: (1) walls, bleachers or other spectator seating areas; (2) team benches and any area behind the team benches; (3) area between the scorer's table and the team benches; (4) any other area outlined in the pre-match conference by the 1st referee.

a. If nets or dividers are separating courts, only the player attempting to play the ball may move the net or divider to play the ball.

b. When competition is scheduled or is occurring on an adjacent court(s), it is a fault for a player to enter the adjacent court(s) to play the ball or after playing the ball. The free zone, including the service zone on an adjacent court, is a playing area. Adjacent courts may not share the same service zone.

9.1 TEAM HITS

A hit is any contact with the ball by a player in play.

The team is entitled to a maximum of three hits (in addition to blocking), for returning the ball. If more are used, the team commits the fault of "FOUR HITS."

9.1.1 CONSECUTIVE CONTACTS

A player may not hit the ball two times consecutively (except Rules 9.2.3, 14.2 and 14.4.2).

9.1.2 SIMULTANEOUS CONTACTS

Two or three players may touch the ball at the same moment.

9.1.2.1 When two or more teammates touch the ball simultaneously, it is counted as one hit. Any player may play the ball next if the simultaneous hit is not the third team hit. If teammates collide, no fault is committed.

9.1.2.2 When two opponents touch the ball simultaneously over the net and the ball remains in play, the team receiving the ball is entitled to another three hits. If such a ball goes "out," it is the fault of the team on the opposite side.

9.1.2.3 If simultaneous hits by two opponents over the net lead to an extended contact with the ball, play continues.

9.1.3 ASSISTED HIT

Within the playing area, a player is not permitted to take support from a teammate or any structure/object in order to hit the ball. However, a player who is about to commit a fault (touch the net or cross the center line, etc.) may be stopped or held back by a teammate.

9.2 CHARACTERISTICS OF THE HIT

9.2.1 The ball may touch any part of the body.

9.2.2 The ball must not be caught and/or thrown. It can rebound in any direction.

9.2.3 The ball may touch various parts of the body, provided that the contacts take place simultaneously.

Exceptions:

9.2.3.1 at blocking, consecutive contacts may be made by one or more player(s), provided that the contacts occur during one action;

9.2.3.2 at the first hit of the team, the ball may contact various parts of the body consecutively, provided that the contacts occur during one action.

9.3 FAULTS IN PLAYING THE BALL

9.3.1 FOUR HITS: a team hits the ball four times before returning it.

9.3.2 ASSISTED HIT: a player takes support from a teammate or any structure/object in order to hit the ball within the playing area.

9.3.3 CATCH: the ball is caught and/or thrown; it does not rebound from the hit.

9.3.4 DOUBLE CONTACT: a player hits the ball twice in succession or the ball contacts various parts of his/her body in succession.

RULE 10. BALL AT THE NET

10.1 BALL CROSSING THE NET

10.1.1 The ball sent to the opponent's court must go over the net within the crossing space. The crossing space is the part of the vertical plane of the net limited as follows:

10.1.1.1 below, by the top of the net;

10.1.1.2 at the sides, by the antennae, and their imaginary extension;

10.1.1.3 above, by the ceiling.

10.1.2 The ball that has crossed the net plane to the opponent's free zone totally or partly through the external space, may be played back within the team hits, provided that:

10.1.2.1 the opponent's court is not touched by the player;

10.1.2.2 the ball, when played back, crosses the net plane again totally or partly through the external space on the same side of the court. The opponent team may not prevent such action.

In addition to the above, a minimum of 2 m (6'6 3/4") clearance beyond the court equipment on both sides is required.

10.1.3 The ball that is heading toward the opponent's court through the lower space is in play until the moment it has completely crossed the vertical plane of the net.

10.2 BALL TOUCHING THE NET

While crossing the net, the ball may touch it.

10.3 BALL IN THE NET

10.3.1 A ball driven into the net may be recovered within the limits of the three team hits.

10.3.2 If the ball rips the mesh of the net or tears it down, the rally is cancelled and replayed.

RULE 11. PLAYER AT THE NET

11.1 REACHING BEYOND THE NET

11.1.1 In blocking, a player may touch the ball beyond the net, provided that he/she does not interfere with the opponent's play before or during the latter's attack hit.

11.1.2 After an attack hit, a player is permitted to pass his/her hand beyond the net, provided that the contact has been made within his/her own playing space.

11.2 PENETRATION UNDER THE NET

11.2.1 It is permitted to penetrate into the opponent's space under the net, provided that this does not interfere with the opponent's play.

11.2.2 Encroachment into the opponent's court with any part(s) of the body is permitted, provided some part of the body remains either in contact with or directly above the center line, and there is no interference with opponents.

In addition, completely crossing the center line with the foot, feet, or hands, or encroachment with other body parts, must not present a safety hazard to opponents.

11.2.3 A player may enter the opponent's court after the ball goes out of play.

11.2.4 Players may penetrate into the opponent's free zone provided that they do not interfere with the opponent's play.

11.3 CONTACT WITH THE NET

11.3.1 Contact with the net by a player between the antennae, during the action of playing the ball, is a fault. The action of playing the ball includes (among others) take-off, hit (or attempt) and landing safely, ready for a new action.

11.3.2 Players may touch the post, ropes, or any other object outside the antennae, including the net itself, provided that it does not interfere with play.

11.3.3 When the ball is driven into the net, causing it to touch an opponent, no fault is committed.

11.4 PLAYER'S FAULTS AT THE NET

11.4.1 A player touches the ball or an opponent in the opponent's space before or during the opponent's attack hit.

11.4.2 A player interferes with the opponent's play while penetrating into the opponent's space under the net.

11.4.3 A player penetrates into the opponent's court in violation of Rule 11.2.2 above

11.4.4 A player interferes with play by (amongst others):

- touching the net between the antennae or the antenna itself during his/her action of playing the ball,
- using the net between the antennae as a support or stabilizing aid,
- creating an unfair advantage over the opponent by touching the net,
- making actions which hinder an opponent's legitimate attempt to play the ball,
- catching/holding onto the net.

Any player close to the ball as it is played, and who is him/herself trying to play it, is considered in the action of playing the ball, even if no contact is made with it. However, touching the net outside the antenna is not to be considered a fault (except for Rule 9.1.3).

RULE 12. SERVICE

The service is the act of putting the ball into play, by the back-right player, placed in the service zone.

12.1 FIRST SERVICE IN A SET

12.1.1 The first service of the first set, as well as that of the deciding 5th set, is executed by the team determined by the toss.

12.1.2 The other sets will be started with the service of the team that did not serve first in the previous set.

12.2 SERVICE ORDER

12.2.1 The players must follow the service order recorded on the line-up sheet.

12.2.2 After the first service in a set, the player to serve is determined as follows:

12.2.2.1 when the serving team wins the rally, the player (or his/her substitute) who served before, serves again;

12.2.2.2 when the receiving team wins the rally, it gains the right to serve and rotates before actually serving. The player who moves from the front-right position to the back-right position will serve.

12.3 AUTHORIZATION OF THE SERVICE

The 1st referee authorizes the service, after having checked that the two teams are ready to play and that the server is in possession of the ball.

In addition to the above, when playing on a portable playing surface, the server shall have at least part of both feet in contact with the playing surface before the 1st referee authorizes the service. After the 1st referee authorizes the service, if the server steps entirely off the playing surface with one or both feet, it is a service fault (Signal 22). See also USAV 12.4.3.

12.4 EXECUTION OF THE SERVICE

12.4.1 The ball shall be hit with one hand or any part of the arm after being tossed or released from the hand(s).

12.4.2 Only one toss or release of the ball is allowed. Dribbling or moving the ball in the hands is permitted.

12.4.3 At the moment of the service hit or take-off for a jump service, the server must not touch the court (the end line included) or the floor outside the service zone.

After the hit, he/she may step or land outside the service zone, or inside the court.

In addition, the service hit must take place on the playing area.

12.4.4 The server must hit the ball within 8 seconds after the 1st referee whistles for service.

For 14-and-under age groups:

a. The server must contact the ball within 5 seconds after the 1st referee whistles for service.

b. If the ball, after having been tossed or released by the server, lands without touching the player, it is considered a service tossing error.

c. After a service tossing error, the referee must authorize the service again (re-serve) and the server must execute it within the next 5 seconds.

d. One service tossing error is permitted for each service.

12.4.5 A service executed before the referee's whistle is cancelled and repeated.

After the whistle for the service, requests for game interruption, i.e., time-out or substitution, may not be considered until after the ball has been served and the rally completed, including a re-serve. A re-serve is part of a single effort to serve, and no requests will be honored during a re-serve. A request for line-up check is permitted when the result of a rally is a replay.

12.5 SCREENING

12.5.1 The players of the serving team must not prevent their opponent, through individual or collective screening, from seeing the server and the flight path of the ball.

12.5.2 A player or group of players of the serving team make(s) a screen by waving arms, jumping or moving sideways, during the execution of the service, or by standing grouped, and in so doing hides both the server and the flight path of the ball until the ball reaches the vertical plane of the net.

The factors to be weighed when judging whether a screen has occurred are: (a) the relative positions of the players on the serving team; (b) the path of the serve; (c) the speed of the serve; and (d) the trajectory of the serve. If the players of the serving team are positioned close to each other, and the serve passes over these players at a fast, low trajectory, the probability is greater that a screen has occurred. This probability is lower if: (a) the players of the serving team are not positioned close to each other or are attempting to prevent a screen (i.e., bending over); (b) the path of the serve is not over the players; (c) the speed of the serve is slow; or (d) the trajectory of the serve is high.

12.6 FAULTS MADE DURING THE SERVICE

12.6.1 Serving faults.

The following faults lead to a change of service even if the opponent is out of position. The server:

12.6.1.1 violates the service order;

12.6.1.2 does not execute the service properly.

It is a serving fault if the service toss touches any obstruction before the service contact.

12.6.2 Faults after the service hit.

After the ball has been correctly hit, the service becomes a fault (unless a player is out of position) if the ball:

12.6.2.1 touches a player of the serving team or fails to cross the vertical plane of the net completely through the crossing space;

12.6.2.2 goes "out";

12.6.2.3 passes over a screen.

After the ball has been correctly hit, the service becomes a fault if the ball touches any overhead obstruction.

12.7 SERVING FAULTS AND POSITIONAL FAULTS

12.7.1 If the server makes a fault at the moment of the service hit (improper execution, wrong rotational order, etc.) and the opponent is out of position, it is the serving fault which is sanctioned.

12.7.2 Instead, if the execution of the service has been correct, but the service subsequently becomes faulty (goes out, goes over a screen, etc.), the positional fault has taken place first and is sanctioned.

RULE 13. ATTACK HIT

13.1 CHARACTERISTICS OF THE ATTACK HIT

13.1.1 All actions which direct the ball toward the opponent, with the exception of service and block, are considered as attack hits.

13.1.2 During an attack hit, tipping is permitted only if the ball is cleanly hit, and not caught or thrown.

13.1.3 An attack hit is completed at the moment the ball completely crosses the vertical plane of the net or is touched by an opponent.

13.2 RESTRICTIONS OF THE ATTACK HIT

13.2.1 A front-row player may complete an attack hit at any height, provided that the contact with the ball has been made within the player's own playing space (except Rules 13.2.4 and 13.3.6).

13.2.2 A back-row player may complete an attack hit at any height from behind the front zone:

13.2.2.1 at his/her take-off, the player's foot (feet) must neither have touched nor crossed over the attack line;

13.2.2.2 after his/her hit, the player may land within the front zone.

13.2.3 A back-row player may also complete an attack hit from the front zone, if at the moment of the contact a part of the ball is lower than the top of the net.

13.2.4 No player is permitted to complete an attack hit on the OPPONENT'S service, when the ball is in the front zone and entirely higher than the top of the net.

13.3 FAULTS OF THE ATTACK HIT

13.3.1 A player hits the ball within the playing space of the opposing team.

13.3.2 A player hits the ball "out."

13.3.3 A back-row player completes an attack hit from the front zone, if at the moment of the hit the ball is entirely higher than the top of the net.

13.3.4 A player completes an attack hit on the opponent's service, when the ball is in the front zone and entirely higher than the top of the net.

13.3.5 A Libero completes an attack hit if at the moment of the hit the ball is entirely higher than the top of the net.

13.3.6 A player completes an attack hit from higher than the top of the net when the ball is coming from an overhand finger pass by a Libero in his/her front zone.

13.3.7 If an attack-hit fault occurs simultaneously with a blocking fault by the opponents, a double fault is committed, and the rally is replayed.

RULE 14. BLOCK

14.1 BLOCKING

14.1.1 Blocking is the action of players close to the net to intercept the ball coming from the opponent by reaching higher than the top of the net, regardless of the height of the ball contact. Only front-row players are permitted to complete a block, but at the moment of the contact with the ball, a part of the body must be higher than the top of the net.

14.1.2 Block Attempt

A block attempt is the action of blocking without touching the ball.

14.1.3 Completed Block

A block is completed whenever the ball is touched by a blocker.

14.1.4 Collective Block

A collective block is executed by two or three players close to each other and is completed when one of them touches the ball.

14.2 BLOCK CONTACT

Consecutive (quick and continuous) contacts with the ball may occur by one or more blockers, provided that the contacts are made during one action.

14.3 BLOCKING WITHIN THE OPPONENT'S SPACE

In blocking, the player may place his/her hands and arms beyond the net, provided that this action does not interfere with the opponent's play. Thus, it is not permitted to touch the ball beyond the net until an opponent has executed an attack hit.

Blocking the ball beyond the net above the opponent's team area shall be permitted, provided:

a. the block is made after the opponents have hit the ball in such a manner that the ball would, in the 1st referee's judgment, clearly cross the net if not touched by a player, and no member of the attacking team is in a position to make a play on the ball.

b. the ball is falling near the net, and no member of the attacking team could, in the 1st referee's judgment, make a play on the ball.

14.4 BLOCK AND TEAM HITS

14.4.1 A block contact is not counted as a team hit. Consequently, after a block contact, a team is entitled to three hits to return the ball.

14.4.2 The first hit after the block may be executed by any player, including the one who has touched the ball during the block.

14.5 BLOCKING THE SERVICE

To block an opponent's service is forbidden.

14.6 BLOCKING FAULTS

14.6.1 The blocker touches the ball in the OPPONENT'S space either before or simultaneously with the opponent's attack hit.

14.6.2 A back-row player or a Libero completes a block or participates in a completed block.

14.6.3 Blocking the opponent's service.

14.6.4 The ball is sent "out" off the block.

14.6.5 Blocking the ball in the opponent's space from outside the antenna.

14.6.6 A Libero attempts an individual or collective block.

14.6.7: If a blocking fault is committed simultaneously with an attack-hit fault by the opponent, a double fault is committed, and the rally shall be replayed.

14.6.8: A block is the interception of a ball coming from the opponents. Accordingly, it is a double contact fault if a player has successive contacts while using a blocking action when directing a ball toward the opponent during the execution of the second or third team hit.

CHAPTER 5
INTERRUPTIONS, DELAYS AND INTERVALS

RULE 15. INTERRUPTIONS

An interruption is the time between one completed rally and the1st referee's whistle for the next service. The only regular game interruptions are TIME-OUTS and SUBSTITUTIONS.

15.1 NUMBER OF REGULAR GAME INTERRUPTIONS

Each team may request a maximum of two time-outs and a maximum of 12 substitutions per set.

15.2 SEQUENCE OF REGULAR GAME INTERRUPTIONS

15.2.1 Request for one or two time-outs, and one request for substitution by either team may follow one another, within the same interruption.

15.2.2 However, a team is not authorized to make consecutive requests for substitution during the same interruption. Two or more players may be substituted at the same time within the same request.

15.2.3 There must be a completed rally between two separate substitution requests by the same team. (Exception: a forced substitution due to injury or expulsion/disqualification) (15.5.2, 15.7, 15.8)

This rule limits player(s) substitutions to one request during a game interruption. A subsequent request(s) by the same team during the same game interruption will result in an improper request.

15.3 REQUEST FOR REGULAR GAME INTERRUPTIONS

15.3.1 Regular game interruptions may be requested by either the coach or the game captain.

15.3.2 Substitution before the start of a set is permitted and should be recorded as a regular substitution in that set.

15.3.3 Time-outs before the start of a set are permitted.

15.4 TIME-OUTS AND TECHNICAL TIME-OUTS

15.4.1 Time-out requests must be made by showing the corresponding hand signal, when the ball is out of play and before the whistle for service. All requested time-outs last for 30 seconds.

15.4.4 The players may remain on the court or go to the free zone near their team bench. Any member of the team listed on the roster may participate in the time-out. Coaches and non-playing team members may not enter the court.

Referees may direct teams to move to the free zone near their team bench for administrative purposes. Teams may return to the court when permitted by the referees.

15.5 SUBSTITUTION

15.5.1 A substitution is the act by which a player, other than the Libero or his/her replacement player, after being recorded by the scorer, enters the game to occupy the position of another player, who must leave the court at that moment.

15.5.2 When the substitution is enforced through injury to a player in play this may be accompanied by the coach (or game captain) showing the corresponding hand signal.

15.6 LIMITATION OF SUBSTITUTIONS

a. Twelve substitutions are the maximum permitted per team per set. Substitution of one or more players is permitted at the same time.

b. A player in the starting line-up may leave the set and re-enter, but only in his/her previous position in the line-up (Exception 15.7).

c. A substitute may enter a set in the position of a teammate in the starting line-up.

d. Unlimited individual entries by a substitute within the team's allowable 12 substitutions are permitted. Each entry must be in the same position in the line-up.

e. More than one substitute may enter the set in each position.

15.7 EXCEPTIONAL SUBSTITUTION

A player (except the Libero) who cannot continue playing due to injury or illness, should be substituted legally. If this is not possible, the team is entitled to make an EXCEPTIONAL substitution, beyond the limits of Rule 15.6. An exceptional substitution means that any player who is not on the court at the time of the injury/illness, except the Libero, second Libero or their regular replacement player, may be substituted into the game for the injured/ ill player. The substituted injured/ill player is not allowed to re-enter the match.

An exceptional substitution is not counted as an individual entry or as part of the total team substitutions.

Priority for exceptional substitution:

a. by the starter or a substitute who has played in the position of the injured player, or by any substitute who has not already participated in the set;

b. by any substitute on the bench, regardless of position previously played;

c. by the Libero.

15.8 SUBSTITUTION FOR EXPULSION OR DISQUALIFICATION

An EXPELLED or DISQUALIFIED player must be substituted immediately through a legal substitution. If this is not possible, the team is declared INCOMPLETE.

15.9 ILLEGAL SUBSTITUTION

15.9.1 The following substitutes are illegal:

a. player not on the roster;

b. player with illegal number or uniform;

c. exceeds the number of total team substitutions;

d. player expelled or disqualified;

e. player replaced by exceptional substitution.

15.9.2 When a team has made an illegal substitution and the play has been resumed the following procedure shall apply, in sequence:

15.9.2.1 the team is penalized with a point and service to the opponent;

15.9.2.2 the substitution must be rectified;

15.9.2.3 the points scored by the team at fault since the fault was committed are cancelled; the opponent's points remain valid.

a. If the team at fault is receiving and discovery is after the opponents have served, all points previously scored by the offending team shall be retained. The serving team will be awarded a point unless the error is discovered after the serving team has scored a point. In this case, no additional point will be awarded.

b. If it is not possible to determine when the error first occurred and the offending team is serving, only the last point in that term of service will be removed.

15.9.2.4 No substitution will be charged to the team or player(s), even if required to correct the wrong entry. In addition, any player or team substitutions charged at the time of the wrong entry shall be removed from the score sheet as though they had never occurred.

15.10 SUBSTITUTION PROCEDURE

15.10.1 Substitution must be carried out within the substitution zone.

15.10.2 A substitution shall only last the time needed for recording the substitution on the score sheet and allowing entry and exit of the players.

15.10.3

a. The actual request for substitution starts at the moment of the entrance of the substitute player(s) into the substitution zone, ready to play, during an interruption. The coach does not need to make a substitution hand signal except if the substitution is for injury or before the start of the set.
A verbal request for substitution is not acknowledged by the referees. The substitute must enter the substitution zone for the request to be acknowledged, except for a substitution related to an injury.

b. If the player is not ready, the substitution is not granted and the team is sanctioned for a delay.

c. The request for substitution is acknowledged and announced by the scorer or 2nd referee, by use of the buzzer or whistle respectively. The 2nd referee authorizes the substitution.

15.10.4 If a team intends to make simultaneously more than one substitution, all substitute players must enter the substitution zone at the same time to be considered in the same request. In this case, substitutions must be made in succession, one pair of players after another. If one is illegal, the legal one(s) is/are granted and the illegal is rejected and subject to a delay sanction.

Any significant delay between substitutes entering the substitution zone shall result in the team being limited to one substitute.

15.11 IMPROPER REQUESTS

15.11.1 It is improper to request any regular game interruption:

15.11.1.1 during a rally or at the moment of or after the whistle to serve;

15.11.1.2 by a non-authorized team member;

15.11.1.3 for a second substitution by the same team during the same interruption (i.e. before the end of next completed rally), except in the case of injury/illness of a player in play;

15.11.1.4 after having exhausted the authorized number of time-outs and substitutions.

15.11.2 The first improper request by a team in the match that does not affect or delay the game shall be rejected, but it must be recorded on the score sheet without any other consequences.

However, if a change in request is due to a referee's mind change, the request will be honored, and no sanction assessed.

15.11.3 Any further improper request in the match by the same team constitutes a delay.

15.11.4 A request for first or second time-out may be honored immediately subsequent to an improper request for substitution. A proper request for substitution maybe honored immediately subsequent to an improper request for time-out.

RULE 16. GAME DELAYS

16.1 TYPES OF DELAYS

An improper action of a team that defers resumption of the game is a delay and includes, among others:

16.1.1 delaying regular game interruptions;

16.1.2 prolonging interruptions, after having been instructed to resume the game;

16.1.3 requesting an illegal substitution;

16.1.4 repeating an improper request;

16.1.5 delaying the game by a team member.

16.1.6 If a request for an illegal substitution or excess time-out is acknowledged (i.e. whistled) by the referees, a delay sanction shall result. No additional request for game interruption from that team may be made until the next completed rally. Any substitution request that is improper or causes a delay is denied.

16.2 DELAY SANCTIONS

16.2.1 "Delay warning" and "delay penalty" are team sanctions.

16.2.1.1 Delay sanctions remain in force for the entire match.

16.2.1.2 All delay sanctions are recorded on the score sheet.

16.2.2 The first delay in the match by a team member is sanctioned with a "DELAY WARNING."

16.2.3 The second and subsequent delays of any type by any member of the same team in the same match constitute a fault and are sanctioned with a "DELAY PENALTY": a point and service to the opponent.

16.2.4 Delay sanctions imposed before or between sets are applied in the following set.

RULE 17. EXCEPTIONAL GAME INTERRUPTIONS

17.1 INJURY/ILLNESS

17.1.1 Should a serious accident occur while the ball is in play, the referee must stop the game immediately and permit medical assistance to enter the court. The rally is then replayed. If the injured player cannot continue playing within a reasonable amount of time, the player must be replaced by substitution, a legal Libero replacement (if the Libero is not on the court at the time of the injury), or the team must take a legal time-out.

a. If the referees are informed that a substitute will replace the injured player, no time-out will be charged regardless of the time required to safely remove the player from the playing area.

b. No substitution requests may be made by the injured player's team until the injury situation is resolved.

17.1.2 If an injured player is unable to play and a legal or exceptional substitution cannot be made, the referee must grant a special time-out of up to three minutes. Play will be resumed as soon as the injured player is able to continue. In no case shall the special injury time-out exceed three minutes. After the special time-out, a team may request a legal time-out. If, after three minutes, or at the expiration of time-outs granted subsequent to the special time-out, the injured player cannot continue to play, the team is declared incomplete for the set No player may be granted more than one three-minute injury time-out during any match. If a player becomes injured to the extent that a second injury time-out would be required, the team is declared incomplete for the match.

17.2 EXTERNAL INTERFERENCE

If there is any external interference during the game, the play has to be stopped and the rally is replayed.

17.3 PROLONGED INTERRUPTIONS

For tournament play where a court change is necessitated, the match will be continued from the point of the interruption.

17.3.1 If unforeseen circumstances interrupt the match, the 1st referee, the organizer and the Control Committee, if there is one, shall decide the measures to be taken to re-establish normal conditions.

17.3.2 Should one or several interruptions occur, not exceeding 4 hours in total:

17.3.2.1 if the match is resumed on the same playing court, the interrupted set shall continue normally with the same score, players (except expelled or disqualified ones) and positions. The sets already played will keep their scores;

17.3.2.2 If the match is resumed on another playing court, the interrupted set shall continue normally with the same score, players (except expelled or disqualified ones) and positions. The sets already played will keep their scores.

17.3.3 Should one or several interruptions occur, exceeding 4 hours in total, the whole match shall be replayed.

RULE 18. INTERVALS AND CHANGE OF COURTS

18.1 INTERVALS

An interval is the time between sets. All intervals last 3 minutes. During this period of time, the change of courts and line-up registrations of the teams on the score sheet are made.

The interval between the second and the third set can be extended up to 10 minutes by the competent body at the request of the organizer.

18.2 CHANGE OF COURTS

18.2.1 After each set, the teams change courts, with the exception of the deciding set.

18.2.2 In the deciding set, once the leading team reaches 8 points, the teams change courts without delay and the player positions remain the same. If the change is not made once the leading team reaches 8 points, it will take place as soon as the error is noticed. The score at the time that the change is made remains the same.

CHAPTER 6
THE LIBERO PLAYER

RULE 19. THE LIBERO PLAYER

19.1 DESIGNATION OF THE LIBERO

19.1.1 Each team has the right to designate from the list of players on the score sheet (roster) up to two specialized defensive players called Liberos. If the team chooses to designate two Liberos at the start of the match, they are designated as Liberos for the entire match. If the team chooses to designate only one Libero (or no Libero) at the start of the match, the team may choose to change the player designated as Libero for each set including playing any set with no Libero, but may not designate a second Libero for any subsequent set in the match.

19.1.2 All Liberos must be recorded on the score sheet in the special lines reserved for this.

19.1.3 The Libero on court is the Acting Libero. If there is another Libero, he/she is the second Libero for the team. Only one Libero may be on court at any time.

19.2 EQUIPMENT

a. The Libero must wear a jersey that clearly contrasts with the jersey of their teammates.

b. A jacket or bib can only be worn by the re-designated Libero. If a jacket or bib is worn by the re-designated Libero, the uniform number must still be visible.

c. Numbers shall be a contrasting color to the uniform top and meet all other specifications in USAV 4.3.3.1. Color combinations such as purple/black, dark green/black, navy/maroon, and white/light yellow are not distinctive enough to comply with the rules. The color of the number must clearly contrast with the color of the jersey irrespective of any border around the number.

19.3 ACTIONS INVOLVING THE LIBERO

19.3.1 The playing actions:

19.3.1.1 the Libero is allowed to replace any player in a back-row position;

19.3.1.2 he/she is restricted to perform as a back-row player and is not allowed to complete an attack hit from anywhere (including playing court and free zone) if at the moment of the contact the ball is entirely higher than the top of the net;

19.3.1.3

a. The Libero may not block or attempt to block.

b. In one position a Libero may serve after replacing the player in position 1.

19.3.1.4 a player (teammate) may not complete an attack hit when the ball is entirely higher than the top of the net, if the ball is coming from an overhand finger pass by a Libero in his/her front zone. The ball may be freely attacked if the Libero makes the same action from outside his/her front zone.

19.3.2 LIBERO REPLACEMENTS

19.3.2.1 Libero replacements are not counted as substitutions. They are unlimited but there must be a completed rally between two Libero replacements (unless a penalty causes the team to rotate and the Libero to move to position four, or the Acting Libero becomes unable to play, making the rally incomplete).

In one rotation, a Libero can replace the player in position 1 and serve the next rally, even if he/she is already on the court in replacement of another player. In this situation, the Libero does not have to exit the court before replacing the player in position 1, and there does not need to be a completed rally between Libero replacements.

19.3.2.2 The regular replacement player may replace and be replaced by either Libero.

The Acting Libero can only be replaced by the regular replacement player for that position or by the second Libero.

19.3.2.3 At the start of each set, the Libero cannot enter the court until the 2nd referee has checked the line-up and authorized a Libero replacement with a starting player.

19.3.2.4 Other Libero replacements must only take place while the ball is out of play and before the whistle for service.

19.3.2.5 A Libero replacement made after the whistle for service but before the service hit should not be rejected; however, at the end of the rally, the game captain must be informed that this is not a permitted procedure, and that repetition will be subject to delay sanctions.

19.3.2.6 Subsequent late Libero replacements shall result in the play being interrupted immediately, and the imposition of a delay sanction. The team to serve next will be determined by the level of the delay sanction.

19.3.2.7 The Libero and the replacing player may only enter or leave the court through the Libero Replacement Zone.

19.3.2.8 Libero replacements must be recorded on the Libero Control Sheet (if one is used) or on the electronic score sheet.

19.3.2.9 An illegal Libero replacement can involve (amongst others):

- no completed rally between Libero replacements;
- the Libero being replaced by a player other than the second Libero or the regular replacement player.
  An illegal Libero replacement should be considered in the same way as an illegal substitution: i.e. should the illegal Libero replacement be noticed before the start of the next rally, then this is corrected by the referees, and the team is sanctioned for delay; should the illegal Libero replacement be noticed after the service hit, the consequences are the same as for an illegal substitution.

19.4 RE-DESIGNATION OF A NEW LIBERO

19.4.1 The Libero becomes unable to play if injured, ill, expelled or disqualified.

The Libero may be declared unable to play for any reason by the coach or, in the absence of a coach, by the game captain.

19.4.2 Team with one Libero

19.4.2.1 When only one Libero is available for a team according to Rule 19.4.1, or the team has only one registered, and this Libero becomes or is declared unable to play, the coach (or game captain if no coach is present) may re-designate as Libero for the remainder of the match any other player (replacement player excepted) not on the court at the moment of the re-designation.

19.4.2.2 If the Acting Libero becomes unable to play, he/she may be replaced by the regular replacement player or immediately and directly to court by a re-designated Libero. However, a Libero who is the subject of a re-designation may not play for the remainder of the match. If the Libero is not on court when declared unable to play, he/she may also be the subject of a re-designation. The Libero declared unable to play may not play for the remainder of the match.

19.4.2.3 The coach, or game captain if no coach is present, contacts the second referee informing him/her about the re-designation.

19.4.2.4 Should a re-designated Libero become or be declared unable to play, further re-designations are permitted.

19.4.2.5 If the coach requests the team captain to be re-designated as the new Libero, this will be permitted and the team captain retains all leadership privileges.

19.4.2.6 In the case of a re-designated Libero, the number of the player re-designated as Libero must be recorded on the score sheet remarks section and on the Libero control sheet (or electronic score sheet if one is used).

19.4.3 Team with two Liberos

19.4.3.1 Where a team has registered on the score sheet two Liberos, but one becomes unable to play the team has the right to play with only one Libero. No re-designation will be allowed, however, unless the remaining Libero is unable to continue playing for the match.

19.5 SUMMARY

19.5.1 If the Libero is expelled or disqualified, he/she may be replaced immediately by the team's second Libero. Should the team have only one Libero, then it has the right to make a re-designation.

CHAPTER 7
PARTICIPANTS' CONDUCT

RULE 20. REQUIREMENTS OF CONDUCT

20.1 SPORTSMANLIKE CONDUCT

20.1.1 Participants must know and abide by the FIVB Official Volleyball Rules and the USA Volleyball modifications to those rules.

20.1.2 Participants must accept referees' decisions with sportsmanlike conduct, without disputing them. In case of doubt, clarification may be requested only through the game captain.

20.1.3 Participants must refrain from actions or attitudes aimed at influencing the decisions of the referees or covering up faults committed by their team.

20.2 FAIR PLAY

20.2.1 Participants must behave respectfully and courteously in the spirit of FAIR PLAY, not only toward the referees, but also toward other officials, the opponent, teammates and spectators.

20.2.2 Communication between team members during the match is permitted.

RULE 21. MISCONDUCT AND ITS SANCTIONS

21.1 MINOR MISCONDUCT

Minor misconduct offenses are not subject to sanctions. It is the 1st referee's duty to prevent the teams from approaching the sanctioning level. This is done in two stages:

Stage 1: by issuing a verbal warning through the game captain; Stage 2: by use of a YELLOW CARD to the team member(s) concerned. This formal warning is not in itself a sanction but a symbol that the team member (and by extension the team) has reached the sanctioning level for the match. It is recorded in the score sheet but has no immediate consequences.

Note: Yellow card warnings are assessed to individuals but are in force for the entire team. This means each team may receive only one yellow card per match.

21.2 MISCONDUCT LEADING TO SANCTIONS

Incorrect conduct by a team member toward officials, opponents, teammates or spectators is classified in three categories according to the seriousness of the offense.

21.2.1 Rude conduct: action contrary to good manners or moral principles.

21.2.2 Offensive conduct: defamatory or insulting words or gestures or any action expressing contempt.

21.2.3 Aggression: actual physical attack or aggressive or threatening behavior.

21.3 SANCTION SCALE

According to the judgment of the 1st referee and depending on the seriousness of the offense, the sanctions to be applied and recorded on the score sheet are: Penalty, Expulsion or Disqualification.

21.3.1 Penalty

The first rude conduct in the match by any team member is penalized with a point and service to the opponent.

21.3.2 Expulsion

21.3.2.1 A team member who is sanctioned by expulsion shall not play for the rest of the set, must be substituted legally and immediately if on court and must remain seated in the penalty area with no other consequences. An expelled coach loses his/her right to intervene in the set and must remain seated in the penalty area.

When facility space does not allow for a penalty area, a player or substitute who is sanctioned by expulsion shall not play for the rest of the set and must remain seated on his/her bench for the remainder of the set. Any other team member sanctioned by expulsion must leave the playing area, bench and warm-up area for the remainder of the set and loses his/her right to intervene in the set.

21.3.2.2 The first offensive conduct by a team member is sanctioned by expulsion with no other consequences.

21.3.2.3 The second rude conduct in the same match by the same team member is sanctioned by expulsion with no other consequences.

21.3.3 Disqualification

21.3.3.1 A team member who is sanctioned by disqualification must be substituted legally and immediately if on court and must leave the Competition-Control Area for the rest of the match with no other consequences.

For the purposes of a disqualification, the Competition Control Area described above includes, at a minimum, the playing area, bench, warm-up area and spectator area.

21.3.3.2 The first physical attack or implied or threatened aggression is sanctioned by disqualification with no other consequences.

21.3.3.3 The second offensive conduct in the same match by the same team member is sanctioned by disqualification with no other consequences.

21.3.3.4 The third rude conduct in the same match by the same team member is sanctioned by disqualification with no other consequences.

21.4 APPLICATION OF MISCONDUCT SANCTIONS

21.4.1 All misconduct sanctions are individual sanctions, remain in force for the entire match and are recorded on the score sheet.

21.4.2 The repetition of misconduct by the same team member in the same match is sanctioned progressively (the team member receives a heavier sanction for each successive offense).

21.4.3 Expulsion or disqualification due to offensive conduct or aggression does not require a previous sanction.

21.5 MISCONDUCT BEFORE AND BETWEEN SETS

Any misconduct occurring before or between sets is sanctioned according to Rule 21.3 and sanctions apply in the following set.

21.6 SUMMARY OF MISCONDUCT AND CARDS USED

Warning: no sanction –

Stage 1: verbal warning

Stage 2: symbol Yellow card

Penalty: sanction – symbol Red card

Expulsion: sanction – symbol Red + Yellow cards jointly

Disqualification: sanction – symbol Red + Yellow card separately

SECTION II

ORDER OF THE RULES

THE REFEREES, THEIR RESPONSIBILITIES & OFFICIAL HAND SIGNALS

USAVolleyball

CHAPTER 8
REFEREES

RULE 22. REFEREEING CORPS AND PROCEDURES

22.1 COMPOSITION

The refereeing corps for a match is composed of the following officials:

- the 1st referee;
- the 2nd referee;
- the scorer;
- the assistant scorer;
- four (two) line judges.

Their location is shown in Diagram 10.

22.2 PROCEDURES

22.2.1 Only the 1st and 2nd referees may blow a whistle during the match:

In addition to the referees, the scorer may use an audible device, including a whistle, to notify the referees of a rotational fault.

22.2.1.1 the 1st referee gives the signal for the service that begins the rally;

22.2.1.2 the 1st or 2nd referee signals the end of the rally, provided that they are sure that a fault has been committed and they have identified its nature.

22.2.2 They may blow the whistle when the ball is out of play to indicate that they authorize or reject a team request.

22.2.3 Immediately after the referee's whistle to signal the completion of the rally, they have to indicate with the official hand signals:

22.2.3.1 If the fault is whistled by the 1st referee, he/she will indicate in order:

a. the team to serve;

b. the nature of the fault;

c. he player(s) at fault (if necessary).

d. the 2nd referee will follow the 1st referee's hand signals by repeating them.

22.2.3.2 If the fault is whistled by the 2nd referee, he/she will indicate:

a. the nature of the fault;

b. the player at fault (if necessary);

c. the team to serve following the hand signal of the 1st referee. In this case, the 1st referee does not show either the nature of the fault or the player at fault, but only the team to serve.

22.2.3.3 In the case of an attack hit fault or blocking fault by back-row or Libero players, both referees indicate according to 22.2.3.1 and 22.2.3.2 above.

22.2.3.4 In the case of a double fault both referees indicate in order:

a. the nature of the fault;

b. the players at fault (if necessary).

The team to serve next is then indicated by the 1st referee.

RULE 23. 1ST REFEREE

23.1 LOCATION

The 1st referee carries out his/her functions standing on a referee's stand located at one end of the net on the opposite side to the scorer. His/her view must be approximately 50 cm (19½") above the net.

23.2 AUTHORITY

23.2.1 The 1st referee directs the match from the start until the end. He/she has authority over all members of the refereeing corps and the members of the teams. During the match his/her decisions are final. He/she is authorized to overrule the decisions of other members of the refereeing corps, if it is noticed that they are mistaken. He/she may even replace a member of the refereeing corps who is not performing his/her functions properly.

23.2.2 He/she also controls the work of the ball retrievers, floor wipers and moppers.

23.2.3 He/she has the power to decide any matters involving the game, including those not provided for in the rules.

23.2.4 He/she shall not permit any discussion about his/her decisions.

However, at the request of the game captain, the 1st referee will give an explanation on the application or interpretation of the rules upon which he/she has based the decision. If the game captain does not agree with this explanation and chooses to protest against such decision, he/she must do so immediately by following the Protest Procedures in USAV 5.1.2.1.

23.2.5 The 1st referee is responsible for determining before and during the match whether the playing area equipment and the conditions meet playing requirements.

23.3 RESPONSIBILITIES

23.3.1 Prior to the match, the 1st referee:

23.3.1.1 inspects the conditions of the playing area, the balls and other equipment;

23.3.1.2 performs the toss with the team captains;

23.3.1.3 controls the teams' warming up.23.3.2 During the match, he/she is authorized:

23.3.2.1 to issue warnings to the teams;

23.3.2.2 to sanction misconduct and delays;

23.3.2.3 to decide upon:

a. the faults of the server and of the positions of the serving team, including the screen;
b. the faults in playing the ball;
c. the faults above the net, and the faulty contact of the player with the net, primarily on the attacker's side;
d. the attack hit faults of the Libero and back- row players;
e. the completed attack hits made by a player on a ball above net height coming from an overhand pass with fingers by the Libero in his/her front zone;
f. the ball crossing completely the lower space under the net;
g. the completed block by back-row players or the attempted block by the Libero.
h. the ball that crosses the net totally or partly outside of the crossing space to the opponent's court or contacts the antenna on his/her side of the playing court.
i. the served ball and the third hit passing over or outside the antenna on his/her side of the court.

23.3.3 At the end of the match, he/she checks the score sheet and signs it.

RULE 24. 2ND REFEREE

24.1 LOCATION

The 2nd referee performs his/her functions standing outside the playing court near the post, on the opposite side of and facing the 1st referee.

24.2 AUTHORITY

24.2.1 The 2nd referee is the assistant of the 1st referee, but has also his/her own range of jurisdiction. Should the 1st referee become unable to continue his/her work, the 2nd referee may replace him/her.

24.2.2 He/she may, without whistling, also signal faults outside his/her range of jurisdiction, but may not insist on them to the 1st referee.

24.2.3 He/she controls the work of the scorer(s).

24.2.4 He/she supervises the team members on the team bench and reports their misconduct to the 1st referee.

24.2.5 He/she controls the players in the warm-up areas.

24.2.6 He/she authorizes the regular game interruptions, controls their duration and rejects improper requests.

24.2.7

a. The 2nd referee reports substitutions 9, 10, 11 and 12 to the appropriate coach or game captain and reports substitution 12 to the 1st referee.
b. The second referee reports each team's second time-out to the appropriate coach or game captain and to the 1st referee.
c. Failure to report team substitutions or time-outs to the coach or captain is not grounds for a protest.

d. During the match, the coach or captain may request verification of the number of team substitutions or time-outs. If incorrect information is provided by the 2nd referee and the team acts directly upon this misinformation resulting in an illegal substitution (per USAV 15.9.1) or an excessive time-out, the referee's error will be corrected with no penalty or sanction assessed to the team.

e. When a referee incorrectly informs a coach or captain that the team has used all time-outs or team substitutions, but later discovers the information is inaccurate and corrects it, the team has no basis for a protest since teams also have a responsibility to maintain records of their team substitutions and time-outs.

f. When a team acts upon misinformation but the action does not result in an excessive substitution or time-out, the request is considered legal and is not grounds for the team to change or withdraw the request. A delay sanction is assessed if the team withdraws a legal request that has been acknowledged (whistled) by a referee.

24.2.8 In the case of an injury of a player, he/she authorizes an exceptional substitution or grants a 3-minute recovery time.

24.2.9 He/she checks the floor condition, mainly in the front zone. He/she also checks, during the match, that the balls still fulfill the regulations.

24.3 RESPONSIBILITIES

24.3.1 At the start of each set, at the change of courts in the deciding set and whenever necessary, the 2nd referee checks that the actual positions of the players on the court correspond to those on the line-up sheets.

a. The 2nd referee's line-up check prior to the start of any set is a courtesy. It is the responsibility of the captain and/or coach to ensure the players maintain the correct service order once the 2nd referee has completed this line-up check.

b. During the match, the coach or captain may request verification of player positions or may confirm the correct server. If incorrect information is provided by the 2nd referee, and the team acts directly upon this misinformation resulting in a rotational fault (wrong server), the referee's error will be corrected. The point(s) scored by the wrong server will be canceled. The team will be placed in the correct order and will resume serving from the moment the incorrect information was provided. However, if the referee's error is discovered after the opponent has served, the team at fault will retain any points scored and will be placed in the correct order. No additional point will be awarded to the opponent.

24.3.2 During the match, he/she decides, whistles and signals:

24.3.2.1 penetration into the opponent's court, and the space under the net;

24.3.2.2 positional faults of the receiving team;

24.3.2.3 the 2nd referee decides, whistles and signals the the faulty contact of the player with the net and with the antenna on his/her side of the court;

24.3.2.4 the completed block by back-row players or the attempted block by the Libero; or the attack hit fault by back-row players or by the Libero;

The 1st referee may also whistle and signal attack-hit faults of the Libero and back-row players.

24.3.2.5 the contact of the ball with an outside object;

24.3.2.6 the contact of the ball with the floor when the 1st referee is not in position to see the contact;

24.3.2.7 the ball that crosses the net plane totally or partly outside the crossing space to the opponent's court or contacts the antenna on his/her side of the court.

24.3.2.8 the served ball and the 3rd hit passing over or outside the antenna on his/her side of the court.

24.3.3 At the end of the match, he/she is not required to sign the score sheet, but is still required to check the score sheet for accuracy.

RULE 25. SCORER

25.1 LOCATION

The scorer performs his/her functions seated at the scorer's table on the opposite side of the court from and facing the 1st referee.

25.2 RESPONSIBILITIES

He/she fills in the score sheet according to the rules, cooperating with the 2nd referee.

He/she uses a buzzer or other sound device to notify irregularities or give signals to the referees on the basis of his/her responsibilities.

25.2.1 Prior to the match and set, the scorer:

25.2.1.1 records the data of the match and teams, including the numbers of the Libero(s), according to the prescribed procedures; however, the captains and coaches do not sign the score sheet before the match.

25.2.1.2 records the starting line-up of each team from the line-up sheet (or checks the data submitted electronically). If he/she fails to receive the line-up sheets on time, he/she immediately notifies this fact to the 2nd referee.

25.2.2 During the match, the scorer:

25.2.2.1 records the points scored;

25.2.2.2 controls the serving order of each team and indicates any error to the referees immediately after the service hit;

25.2.2.3 is empowered to acknowledge and announce requests for player substitutions by use of the buzzer, controlling their number, and records the substitutions and time-outs, informing the 2nd referee;

25.2.2.4 notifies the referees of a request for regular game interruption that is out of order;

25.2.2.5 announces to the referees the ends of the sets, and the scoring of the 8th point in the deciding set;

25.2.2.6 records misconduct warnings, sanctions and improper requests;

25.2.2.7 records all other events as instructed by the 2nd referee, i.e. exceptional substitutions, recovery time, prolonged interruptions, external interference, re-designation, etc.;

25.2.2.8 in the case of protest, writes on the score sheet a statement on the incident being protested.

25.2.3 At the end of the match, the scorer:

25.2.3.1 records the final result;

25.2.3.2 in the case of protest, with the previous authorization of the 1st referee, writes or permits the team/game captain to write on the score sheet a statement on the incident being protested;

25.2.3.3 The only individuals required to sign the score sheet at the conclusion of the match are the scorer and the 1st referee.

RULE 26. ASSISTANT SCORER

26.1 LOCATION

The assistant scorer performs his/her functions seated beside the scorer at the scorer's table.

26.2 RESPONSIBILITIES

He/she records the replacements involving the Libero. He/she assists with the administrative duties of the scorer's work.

Should the scorer become unable to continue his/her work, the assistant scorer substitutes for the scorer.

26.2.1 Prior to the match and set, the assistant scorer:

26.2.1.1 prepares the Libero control sheet;

26.2.1.2 prepares the reserve score sheet.

26.2.2 During the match, the assistant scorer:

26.2.2.1 records the details of the Libero replacements/re-designations and records all substitutions;

26.2.2.2 notifies the referees of any fault of the Libero replacement by using the buzzer;

26.2.2.3 the 2nd referee is responsible for Technical Time-outs;

26.2.2.4 it is recommended that someone other than the assistant scorer operates the visual scoreboard;

26.2.2.5 checks that the scoreboards agree;

26.2.2.6 if necessary, updates the reserve score sheet and gives it to the scorer.

26.2.3 At the end of the match, the assistant scorer:

26.2.3.1 the assistant scorer does not sign the Libero control sheet or the score sheet.

RULE 27. LINE JUDGES

27.1 LOCATION

If two line judges are used, they stand at the corners of the court closest to the right hand of each referee.

27.2 RESPONSIBILITIES

27.2.1 The line judges perform their functions by using flags (40 X 40 cm) (16" X 16"), to signal:

27.2.1.1 the ball "in" and "out" whenever the ball lands near their line(s);

27.2.1.2 the touches of "out" balls by either team;

27.2.1.3 the ball touching the antenna, the served ball and the third hit of the team crossing the net outside the crossing space, etc.;

27.2.1.4 any player (except the server) stepping outside of his/her court at the moment of the service hit;

27.2.1.5 the foot faults of the server;

27.2.1.6 when a player contacts the top 80cm (32") of either antenna.

27.2.1.7 the ball crossing the net outside the crossing space into the opponent's court or touching the antenna on his/her side of the court.

27.2.2 At the 1st referee's request, a line judge must repeat his/her signal.

RULE 28. OFFICIAL SIGNALS

See the USA Volleyball or FIVB Rules Book, Diagram 11, for official hand signals and their descriptions. The official hand signals are also included in the USA Volleyball Officiating and Scoring Guide.

28.1 REFEREES' HAND SIGNALS

The referees must indicate with the official hand signal the reason for their whistle (the nature of the fault whistled or the purpose of the interruption authorized). The signal has to be maintained for a moment and, if it is indicated with one hand, the hand corresponds to the side of the team which has made the fault or the request.

28.2 LINE JUDGES' FLAG SIGNALS

The line judges must indicate with the official flag signal the nature of the fault called and maintain the signal for a moment.

When flags are not used, the line judges will perform their functions as shown in Diagram 11, Official Hand Signals 9, 14, 15, 22, and 24.